HIS

Shirkendra Jackson

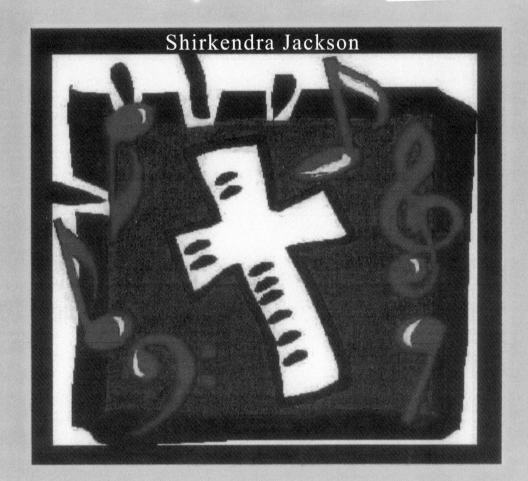

WISDOM

Outskirts Press, Inc.
Denver, Colorado

Outskirts Press, Inc.
http://www.outskirtspress.com

ISBN: 978-1-4327-1912-8

Outskirts Press and the "OP" logo are trademarks belonging to Outskirts Press, Inc.

PRINTED IN THE UNITED STATES OF AMERICA

TABLE OF CONTENTS

ACKNOWLEDGEMENTS

INTRODUCTION

Acknowledgements

Jesus Christ: I would like to take this opportunity to thank my Lord and Savior Jesus Christ for using me to produce His words and His wisdom for my book.
You forever will be my first and most precious love of all!

Mother and Father: I love you both so much for challenging me, pushing me to do my best, and most of all loving me so much to be my parents and my friends. (Lovely sweetie and CCC Action Jackson) All my life you have and always will be a blessing from above.

Michael and Kenneth Jackson Jr.: My brothers you have and always will be my rock to lean on and my strength to stand tall through and through. I truly love you for teaching me not to be afraid of the world! You are my soul survivors! Your generations have already blessed me!

Granny: Thank you so much for your gracious spirit and beautiful smile everyday. Praying diligently for family, my First Pilgrim Missionary Baptist Church. I will never forget how you taught me to truly love God for myself!

Relatives: Through the good and bad times you have made me who I am today. Thank you for your deep roots, your magnificent rainbows of ethnicity, and unconditional love.

Mt Zion Church of Oakwood Village: Thank you Pastor Macon and first family for allowing me to express one of my passions in front of the congregation! To the deacons, ministers, congregation and friends, you are the face of God! I love you!

The House of the Lord: Thank you Minister Trinka Taylor, family and friends for your wonderful testimonies of faith, endurance, courage and strength. The research strategies truly helped me find the right publishing company. God Bless you always!

Suzy Skinner: I knew you were an angel when you stepped into the coffee shop. Your illustrations are a blessing from the Lord. You have touched my life in such a special way. You are my dear sister in Christ. I pray that your light continues to shine. I love you!

Outskirts Press: Thank you for your outstanding publishing qualities, expertise, coaching and acceptance.

Eric A. Weber: Thank you all at PRINT digital inc. for the professional formatting of my illustrations, kindness and efficiency.

Introduction

Shirkendra Lynette Jackson

I was born on January 10th, 1982 in St. Lukes Hospital in Cleveland, Ohio to the proud parents of Shirley and Kenneth Jackson Sr. and my two strong, older brothers Kenneth D. Jackson Jr. and Michael D. Jackson. During the first three innocent years of my life my family and I lived on E. 147th street and St. Clair. Furthermore, I was raised in Macedonia, a pretty nice suburb where *color* was scarce. Fortunately, I had my brothers to help in the transition. All my parents wanted was for us to have a good childhood: one filled with unbelievable faith, dreams and ambitions: Of course, our faith was tested in the school system.

Elementary School seemed to be the perfect community based for anyone, but the outside was very deceiving. The inside made me fill warm and comfortable at first, but the people changed my world of view. The word prejudice became my new vocabulary word, which was taken to the extreme consciousness of isolation from teachers and students. My second grade teacher would force me to realize that I was different by punishing me for false accusations of unacceptable work and behavior. My grades dropped tremendously, my self-esteem became a fantasy that could never be fulfilled. At the age of eight, I wanted to know how it felt to be the most powerful being on the earth. Many times after school I came home crying, asking my mother why *I* was not white.

Furthermore, my parents would have frequent meetings with the principal regarding the matter of prejudential issues. He said we're not used to *"you people"* and teachers are having difficulty dealing with your child's skin color. Meanwhile, my parents struggled daily to find a solution to the dilemma. During one of the meetings, the principal did admit that he had a problem. Unfortunately, we later found out that he committed suicide. Well as time went on, it seemed as though the students had their share in recognizing our differences. I can't remember which one hurt the most: a mixed girl telling me that she didn't like brown people or the teachers punishing me like I was a savage animal on the lose that needed to be neutralized from all humanity.

After the principal's death there were many investigations of how the school system was run. Many other teachers lost their jobs because of the point of view on black students. In fourth grade, challenges were met and changes seemed to be made for the better. Furthermore, music classes were a requirement to learn in order to go to the next grade. With the courage, love and support from my parents and my brothers' own experiences, I found in myself a reason to press through my rainy days. I don't know what spirit the Lord implanted in me, but when I began to sing for the first time, I felt a freedom that I had never felt before. My heart rejoiced with every pitch and note I hit. The choir director was so impressed that he wanted me to do most if not all of the soloist parts. Some of the other students and I competed for a talent show: some played the piano, gymnastics, magic tricks, but I decided to sing my favorite Whitney Houston's song "I Will Always Love You," from the movie Bodyguard. There were those who did doubt me, but to my amazement I actually began to make some friends because of it and they loved hearing me sing. I told my parents that I worked so hard for this and yet again with a loving kiss from my mom and my dad hugging me tightly I knew I could make it threw. That night, I hit every note and got a standing ovation. I may have been a little overweight and my teeth may have not been straight, but I showed it all off in front of the cameras. I felt like I was on top of the world. For once I really think that they understood me for me and not for the color of my skin.

Although I had many trials and tribulations, middle school calmed many of my storms with the use of cross-country and track. Cross-country was so difficult, especially for a 5'3, 140lb chubby girl, but I wanted to feel appreciated so I went for it. I remember every meet we had rain or snow, my lovely mom would be waiting at the finish line yelling at the top of her lungs for me to run faster. Unfortunately, I always came in last or second to last, but seeing my mother put a smile on my face. On the other hand, I found my footing in the 100-meter dash and the 4x4 relay. I felt so good about myself because I earned the Honor Roll in academics and the Muncie Award in track. This proved to me that God grants justice to his people.

Meanwhile, my eyes were really opened to the diversity of other ethnic backgrounds such as Asian, Hispanic, and Native American etc. The devastating drop was the unbelievable control of peer pressure and popularity. A new era of adolescence and curiosity had sprung forth: the light skinned girls were the most popular and early promiscuity seemed to be the norm. I was shocked to know how many early pregnancies and miscarriages were going on around the school. The uncontrollable tempers of the students really frightened me and being the outsider painted a whole new meaning to the word prejudice. It was now black against black, one thinking that behaving like a civil human being and achieving accomplishments made you an Oreo. (Black on the outside but white on the inside). The white students were considered the *smart* ones. Well of course I was in the Oreo category, but I didn't have any indication of thinking the opposite. I found nothing wrong with getting get A's in my classes and just simply following the rules.

Some black students point of view was that we should act as though they would expect us to act: unruly and not capable of learning. Fortunately, I didn't feel that coldness from my teachers; they wanted me to do my best. I struggled so hard to fit in with the crowd, that I lost more friends than gaining any. The teachers were very educational and supportive of all students and they did not single anyone out for their color. They based their judgments on character and discipline.

In 1996, high school was a totally different story. There were about twenty of us and it seemed that not enough love could go around the building. This stage of life was experimental. Everyone thought they were the bomb: The fashion of hip-hop went to another level. The baggy jeans, loose T-shirts, timberlands and wife beaters from the brothers. The preppy rich kids would wear the rah, rah cheerleading outfits which included fitted khakis, tight tank tops with a little sweater. The popularity contest was promiscuity, drinking and violence. Of course I had my so-called circle of girlfriends and our style was Calvin Klein and Guess. They had their way of including me in things that they knew I would put up with. Furthermore, being an outsider or rather goody-goody too-shoes was not an easy job, but I had to show them that having a mind of your own wasn't all that bad. I did however loved dancing every weekend with my girlfriends:

I got my very first job at age fifteen as a server at Boston Market and I felt like a slave cleaning those bathrooms every night, sweeping and moping that dinning room area all by myself and working those ridiculous late hours, so I decided to go to Wal-mart. I guess they didn't care about minors' hours either because during the holidays I would be stocking items until 1:00 a.m. in the morning. Of course, my parents had to speak with the manager and evidently he was having the same problem with every other young worker. Many of us left because of the unfair salary and the mistreatment of our time. My parents decided that it was best to get involved in some school activities.

The extracurricular activities was sometimes fun but then again being singled out didn't always fill so great even though I didn't like what the other crowd was doing or saying. Volleyball was my favorite, but I very rarely got a chance to play. I practiced so hard and I thought that I was good but I wasn't perfect. A sudden tragedy occurred in my big little world that changed my life forever.

My testimony of faith began on January 14th 1998 it was around 2:15 in the afternoon, four days after my 16th birthday, when I found myself learning the foundation of algebra and later that evening around 7:30 or 8:00 I was admitted to the emergency room at South Pointe Meridian Hospital in Sagamore Hills. To my parents' discovery and to a secret that I had been carrying for about a month, was that I had bruises all over my body my skin and eyes were covered with little red dots. The gym teachers would question me wearing sweatpants and sweatshirts and I would lie telling them that I wanted to sweat and stay in shape. (Some thought that I was being abused) I was so angry with myself for hiding the truth. I saw, I just prayed that it would go away without anyone knowing about it! Moreover, my parents and I waited patiently, while various doctors came in and out of the room examining me: neither one could diagnose me with the symptoms that I had. I prayed silently, but my situation only got worse. I began to start hemorrhaging. (I thought to myself goodness I'm going to die at age 16) My mother was crying and my dad seemed like he was keeping it together but the look on his face proved otherwise. Miraculously, I didn't feel any pain just very fatigue. After the examination the nurse escorted us into this small dark room where they inserted an Ivy tube in my arm and before she left she said that I needed to be transported to another hospital immediately and that it wouldn't be long. Three hours went by and I don't know for how long my parents and I prayed that I was okay. I felt a strong force welding me to the bed… I couldn't move, so I just slept. I could feel my mother's hand gently rubbing my head and my back. The doctor came in and said that there was a room available at the Akron Children's Hospital and they could treat me there. Still not knowing what was wrong with me, the doctors' gave us directions and we went.

The next thing I remember I woke up in a hospital robe looking up at the high ceiling, a television to the right of my window and a small lamp next to my bed. My mom called my name and I looked at her while my dad was sitting on the other bed. The doctor was taking more blood out of the other arm this time. I glanced at my left arm with the Ivy and a tiny tube that ran up to a small bag. The doctor told me that I needed to have a blood transfusion because I had lost a lot of blood. The history behind the red blood cells is that it keeps the blood flowing from organ to organ and your spling can sometimes dysfunction in a way that it would eat your red blood cells. That's what causes your blood to stop clotting and form red dots, which in turn will bring your platelet count down below normal: The average count is 150,000 to 350,000. Normal is 450,000 and above. Mine was below 3,000. My immune system was failing which enabled the symptoms that I just mentioned to take its course. I was finally diagnosed with the early stages of Leukemia or Lupus. The doctor then told us that my condition was very uncommon.

Over the course of two weeks, which seemed like two years I was given a prescription called prednoszyone, a steroid that rebuilds the immune system and any damage done to organs. The iron pills were prescribed for the restoration of my red blood cells. The dosage per day for both pills was seven, which was to be eaten with breakfast, lunch I won't even get into the dinner part because it was ridiculous. I kept thinking to myself there is no way I can eat all this food! But the doctor said that the medication was very strong and it required as many nutrients as possible. In addition, I had to have my bone marrow tested for any cancerous activity. My mom was so terrified of how long the needle was but I was sedated: Thank the Lord the test came back negative. But I was almost at my breaking point. I begged my parents to take me home because I couldn't take it anymore! I can't take not walking without help! I can't take being careful of not bumping my head in the shower because I might bleed to death! Lord I'm only sixteen I'm supposed to be having fun! Not lying up in some hospital I'm too young for this! I wanted this trial to be over and done with. When the last day of fourteen days went by the doctor came in the room and said those magic words that only I could have heard in my own way: Shirkendra you can go home your blood count is over 150,000. I was so excited I think I hugged him! All I remember was waiving bye to everyone as they wheeled me to the car.

When we got close to our hometown I wanted to eat everything insight: I ordered two double cheeseburgers, fries and a frosty. (That was the prednozone talking, it makes you eat and gain weight too). A couple of days went by and before I knew I had to go back to school. I couldn't wait to see my few good friends, but something else was very troubling. I realized that my clothes didn't fit me anymore. I remembered going into the hospital weighing 135lbs and came out weighing 198. In addition, I had so much homework to make up and so many quizzes and tests from each of my subjects. Walking became my sport. But by God's grace and mercy, I was able to get B's in all of my classes. I could never have thanked my family enough for their sacrifices, love and support to get through that very difficult but yet durable ordeal. I was celebrating the passing of a good storm!

Furthermore, my college years at Ohio State were the best and worst years of my life. I remembered how excited I was leaving home and not having a curfew. My friends and I went to the freshman welcome parties, where the fraternities and sororities showed their stuff! While getting ready for a football game I would always hear the OH-IO chant. Not a day went by that I didn't see at least a dozen students wearing Ohio State gear. I felt proud to belong to something that stood for excellence in education, morals and respect. I also loved how diverse the campus was: Learning the cultures of others and how they live was so fulfilling. Furthermore, I was involved in many organizations such as Martin Luther King Community Day, Minority Scholarship Program, the Heritage Festival, and the Sigma Sorority Fashion Show.

I interned with Third Federal Savings for two years, where I tried to apply the training to my major in business. I thought it was a great opportunity to work in the Loan Processing, Underwriting and Appraisal department. I was able to apply the work there to the work in my major in college. The last two years of college were very challenging because I had to figure out what I really wanted to do. My GPA wasn't high enough to be accepted into the business college, so I decided to change my major to English with a minor in Communications. Meanwhile, my new major really made me buckle down and concentrate because I had more classes to complete than I already had with business. Thank the Lord that some of those classes were compatible with the English courses, so I wouldn't have to take them over again. Moreover, I felt that this was the time to improve myself and the school that I could make it through!

My coming out of the storm was my graduation on June 13, 2004. The ceremony lasted about 3 ½ scorching, humid hours in those black robes! The director of my college handed me my scarlet diploma with the Ohio State University emblem written in gold on front. I opened it and it read Bachelors in the College of Humanities with a degree in English and a minor in Communications. My emotions took hold of me and I could not stop crying. I remembered that this day may not have come and all of the critics who said that I wouldn't make it in time and that I was over my head were oh so wrong! I was among the 6400 students running across the football stadium with my diploma held high and screaming along with the other graduates. Outside the stadium I was met with my friends and family who cried tears of joy along with me.

Furthermore, getting a job was not at all the easiest of things to accomplish! The market was very competitive and I guess they were not ready for thousands of graduates to take over! With dozens of decline letters from respectable employments and no calls I was feeling a little depressed and realized that I had to find something soon. (Something is better than nothing) I eventually got a job with Target as a customer service representative earning a dollar above minimum wage. Some people thought I was crazy and I thought I was too, but God's ways are not always our ways. He wanted to humble me just a little while longer before he blessed me with an office. I began working at Dollar Bank December 6, 2004 as a Customer Service Representative. The Lord knew that at age 23, I would have no insurance so he gave me some through my employment and also enough money to afford an apartment in Cuyahoga Falls, Ohio, where I currently reside.

In conclusion, I hope that you will enjoy the wisdom and joy that I have captured from above and keep them with you forever. My story was not intended to boast or be the center of attention, but only to open your minds to things that this world has proved to be impossible. What they fail to realize is that with Jesus anything and all things are possible. The Lord says "knock, ask, seek and ye shall find… Whatever ye ask in my name, your faith shall open the windows of heaven and pour you out a blessing that ye shall not have room enough to receive." He has and continues to do that for me and I know he will do that for you… just believe! Be conquered by His love!

God Bless You!

Family

Chapter 1

Mother

The precious scent of perfume
The whole heart of a stranger catering to one's needs
The endless love and compassion with every kiss
The moments of despair washed away with every embrace
The joy of comfort staring into the blooming eyes of a prosperous rose
The smile of an angel after birthing the Lord's creation
The beautiful billows of clouds, caressed with the rising and setting of the sun
The gracious wings of a warrior
The expertise of knowledge
The appreciation is granted to you my dear mother
Your passion shines through and through

Father

The first love of my life here on earth
The light and fire in my eye
As a little girl you would always cater to my aches and pains
As a grown woman you still and will always be God's vessel in
protecting my heart
Your unconditional love has disciplined me to
thrive towards my wildest dreams
Your prayers give me peace and joy
I am so blessed to have you as my guiding light
when even the brightest light can seem so dim
You have given me wisdom and strength to follow through
The honor and dedication is to you, my dear father
Your little girl truly admires and adores you

Father

The first leading man in my life
The light and fire in my eye
As a little boy you would always cater to my aches and pains
As a grown man you still and will always be God's vessel in
protecting my integrity
Your unconditional love has disciplined me to
thrive towards my wildest dreams
Your prayers give me peace and joy
I am so blessed to have you as my guiding light
when even the brightest light can seem so dim
You have given me wisdom and strength to follow through
The honor and dedication is to you, my dear father
Your son truly loves and respects you

Friendship

We share such a strong bond that even the distance cannot bare
Your sweet, understanding words soothes the everyday pain of life's struggles
Your undivided attention lets me know you care
You've been there when no one else cared
Your belief in me gives me encouragement and strength
You accept me for who I am
You accept me for what I have and will become
Your unconditional love has given me freedom to live
Freedom to express my true identity without fear
Freedom to share my story to the young and old
Freedom to take on the world with you as my anchor
My dear brother and sister I thank the Lord for a friend like you
Your spirit shines on my cloudy days
You are perfect in all your ways
Every night and every day you know I'll always pray
For you to always stay

Strength

Chapter 2

Confusion

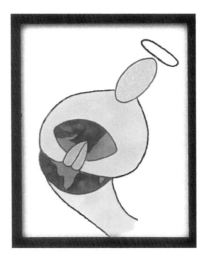

The truth hurts my heart like the lost of a child's first pet
Death, destruction, chaos and madness
We view this other planet and its agonizing crime scenes through our television
We glide through our daily routines, none of these things ever to be seen
The world is sugar coded with strawberries and cream
The tangible things taken for granted is one of the treats hoped for in some European dreams
One average human being could never believe the horror of a child worshiping a gun like it was his
favorite toy
"The land of the free"
The most powerful nation crumbling lot by lot
Inheritance gained by some of the ancient scholars, greed and war
Our country's shelter defeated by the unprotected seashores
North versus South
East versus West
Where did we go wrong?
Have all of our fallen heroes risked their
Lives for families to grow farther and farther apart
For valuable opportunities to missed by future scholars

Because some of our teachers encourage be littleness
Why do we face the fear of youngsters climbing the ladder of success?
Why don't we have the time or the energy to guide them to joyous heights?
We must understand
If they don't achieve greater success
Then this generation will become nonexistence
The cures for us will be in vain
The voices of the lonely and the innocent will never be heard
"In God We Trust"
The most powerful slogan ever used to claim victory
However never being used for its true purpose
The conflict between church and state has never been gratified
Improper man power has caused chaos, madness, destruction and death
Who can turn our past faults around and restore peace in our land?
We know whom we must trust

Lost

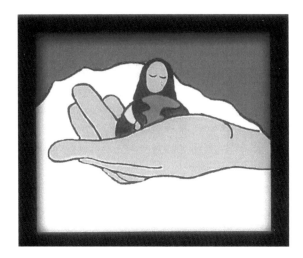

He sees no more, this poor little innocent abandoned child
What really goes on in the mind of a child?
It cries, squeals and yearns for your love
"Eventually it will stop, said the mother
then I won't have to worry anymore."
"What about me says the little child, I can't walk nor crawl, eat or fend for myself!
How can you just leave me?"
Silence
"What happened…? I have blessed you with the perfect gift, a child in your own image, first birthed from me.
You left him in the cold, dark lonely world.
What was he to do?"
"I have nothing Lord, it was a mistake, I have nothing to offer!" said the mother
"My child, I love you unconditionally even through your sins *you* are my most precious and beautiful creation!
I knew you before you were born
I knew what your dreams and aspirations were
I felt the pain of losing a loved one before you emerged from your mother's womb

I watched and nurtured your entire being

I have birthed a king of nations into your womb not to hurt you, but to remind you that you are royalty and I have put in you the proper tools to raise such a child"

"Oh Lord the world, the world is so cruel they won't accept a bastard kid!"

No my child I'm a mother for the motherless, a father for the fatherless. He is my son and my grace and mercy shall change this world. My people just have to realize that I am the way and the truth."

"I have extended my love, strength and wisdom into this child and you must guide him in carrying My joy.

Rise my child, go and get your baby out of the dumpster

I've been with you thus far and I shall never leave you nor forsake your little one

Now nurture, listen, watch, fast and pray and I shall do the rest."

Yes

A Day's Journey

One might not have noticed
How much time was lost
Morning after morning
Day after day
The routine began…
Lost in the sinful streets
No one would take me in
Praying night and day was always the trend
The daily struggles of wearing the veil of destruction and despair finally toke its toll
The reflection of this repulsive creature revealed my true being
Every one went to the alter to pray for John
The Lord answered his prayers for a wife, kids and a great job
Every dream and aspiration was fulfilled
Suddenly disaster struck and the pain would never be healed
The role for the husband was to provide, but something was missing
Before John knew it his daughter was dating at thirteen
His son was in juvenile court for domestic violence against his teacher

His wife finding every excuse not to come home at night
Where did he lose track
This situation happens all too common to the average man
The influence of frequent meetings with the boss
The constant out of town and million dollar client seminars
The trauma hit John so hard that he went to church for the first time after twenty years
He listened closely to the sermon about selfishness
He remembered how depressed he felt
Following the same routine of selling drugs for his father
He thought of his children
"I've been given a chance to guide my children on the right paths in life!
I can't let them go through what I did.
"My mother left my father, but I can't punish my wife by
withholding my heart from her."
Morning after morning
Day after day
Lost in his own world
He threw up his hands surrendering to God once more
John testified that morning in front of his family and friends
He knew who he was and who he wanted to be to his family
For the first time

My Soul

The lost of your inner being trying desperately to find its place
For that split second you are the core of the world
But the world does not care about healing your wounds
You use the moon as your guiding light
The body of Christ as your shield
The stars as your inspiration
The shape of the clouds as a map to your destiny
The closing of one door with the night
The opening of another with the rising of the Son
Your eyes can see His glorious works
But yet their faith is still based on *this* time zone
The Promise Land was and still is fulfilled to everyone
The prophesies have been taught, they live in you
Seek and ye shall find your glorious purpose
Exercise it not for the anointing of your own, but for
the wanderers and the followers searching
high and low for the hopeful One
Utilize your gifts for the kingdom of heaven
We all shall find everlasting rest in the
hands of our Master

Faith

Chapter 3

Fallen Grace

The air was crisp with the morning sunshine
The formation of the clouds guided my footsteps into that sweet aroma café
The crowd was gracious and peaceful
The gentlemen handed me my cup
The soothing whipped cream melted my heart
The caramel raptures my taste buds while the steaming cocoa calms my spirits
I gently closed my eyelids just to enjoy the senses but something else caught my attention
Staring out the window, I saw the busyness of the world growing minute by minute
I quickly glanced down at my watch and to my amazement I only had fifteen minutes left
The mother cried out for her little one Eva! Eva!!
The business man with the cellular phone and briefcase in hand sprints down
Memory lane, while the wanderer watches his every move
The mother watches in horror when the bum grabs the little girl from crossing the intersection
Somebody help! He's kidnapping my baby! Lord save her!
The man in the sharp suit saw him and went for the baby…
"I saw you got to her first? That's' not how its always been."
The precious faith of the mother arose me when she sacrificed her sin this morning
Even when you walked with my Father you were always sly as a snake

"Master, who do you think they will believe in?
The clean, cut man or senseless bum?"
Fifteen minutes seemed to turn into an hour I couldn't believe what I was observing
Don't forget that I use the weakness for strength and power
They shall rule with my Father in His kingdom
"The obstacles of reality have embraced your so-called weakness
The strong will obviously murder them because of fear"
You know how the story ends Clever
The hour has come where I have caught you at your last stance!
I have enwrapped my army of faith against you!
"How did this come about so soon?"
The faith of many but one in particular really completed the mission
The one observing from a far in the coffee shop
The server of multiple mochas and frappichinos
The single mother's love for this child shall make them all brides in my kingdom
Ordinary, weak and low compared to your world
But they are victorious and have pure mansions in mine
They have put together the final pieces of the kingdom
Clever, I'm not impressed with how you twist my words for fashion
You can't deny my TRUTH
Even you and your followers shall bow to my presence
Your hour of damnation has come
You've read the book and you know what happens next
"Fallen Grace was something I once knew"
Yes but remember I have given you the privilege to reign in your own
Children, follow my path: we are forevermore
Amen

If you were and If you are

A Prostitute	A Thief
A Drug Dealer	A Robber
A Crack Baby	A Sex addict
A Child Molester	An Adulterer
A Murderer	A Compulsive
An Abuser	Gambler
A Liar	A Homosexual

If this was all the world judged of you... Then you should know that, your heavenly
Father Jesus Christ knows your past, present and future. So come to Him as you
are and He will provide, what shall be.
The world does not know your warm heart, your compassionate soul and
most of all God's love for you and I. He's all the power you need.
Remember my friend, we are all sinners climbing up the
rough side of the mountain to paradise. So let's
praise and worship Him together hand in
hand because unlike the world, God's
love is not limited to the rich,
famous and high mighty.
He conquers
All!

19

Rise

We say we have pride, but what about the unconditional love?
We scream, shout and complain, but everything still remains the same.

We fight with our mouths, but when asked to face our fears our souls become mute.
We put blame on the majority of the world, but the reason behind our stupidity is isolation

When will we rise?
When will we free ourselves to love?
Instead of being forbidden by pride and hatred
Whose children will look up to this selfish society?
Every man for himself
Every child to fend for themselves
Another child goes off the edge
Another finger pointed
One more guilty conscience
One more unsolved crime
Unforgettable memories
Unforgettable photographs of what could have been
Do we give ourselves time to wonder about the who and the when
Why do we wait for the swiftness of existence to pass away?
When will we really see?
When will we rise?

Heroism

Chapter 4

My son, my daughter
My hero

The Lord has called you
He has called you for one of the greatest assignments you may ever have to face
To defend your country
I too my child have questioned my Savior about putting you into such fatal danger
But I do remember what the Lord allowed his son Jesus to endure for our souls to be set free
Jesus is in you now always
You must pick up your daily cross and walk
Carry the Father, the Son and the Holy Spirit in your heart
Through combat follow the path of Jesus
He is the true and only judge of all nations
Believe me I feel your wounds of despair, unimaginable agony and trauma
I kneel by my bedside every night praying for your safe return
Don't worry it will be over soon my child
Through battle the Lord shall command your army with the armor of grace and mercy
He shall wrap His protective arms around you when the enemy entraps you
He has not forgotten you my child
This is your journey, your time to shine

You have made me so proud
I'm so blessed to have birthed such an incredible being into this world
A being that has brought light into my life and to so many others
You are my inspiration
God's vessel to carry on day after day

The Virtuous Woman

Dear Women of Christ,

The sunshine caresses your silken nature
The moon shadows the indigo of your glorious past
Each and every day is a day for us to remember
the most precious gift of all…
when you gazed into our sparkling eyes at birth
Words cannot express the freedom we now enjoy because of your
journey of pain, but yet not in vain your sacrifices
You have graced us with you presence of joy, love and power
Instilled your wondrous works of praise
only for us to press through our rainy days
Proverbs 31:25, "Strength and honor are her clothing…"
Strength to conquer humanity
Honor to lift us higher
Through war you have fought with faith for our blessings to flow
You are the survivor of all things

We listen to your wisdom of praise, stroll your path of righteousness
My dear sisters, we thank you for paving the way
for our voices to be heard and appreciated
We now follow the footsteps that you
placed before your beloved daughters
We shall continue your everlasting beauty of
virtuous harmony

My lovely sisters
For such a time as this…
Rise, Rise and be recognized
God Bless

Joy

Chapter 5

Jazz

Some may come, some may go
Love will come but love will never go
The true love, the love of my life
You romance me with your sweet precious kiss
Your embrace captures my heart and wraps it around your presence
My destiny lies within your soul
Your rhythm propels my adrenaline
Your art sets my skin on fire
Your desire intrigues me to perform
The swiftness of my feet
The magic wand of my arms
The salsa of my hips
Your dream is in my walk
You are beautiful…
Let me express it
Dance with me

Dream

I remember our past thoughts and visions of that heavenly world
We would try our best to prepare
My love, where have you gone?
It seemed as if it were only yesterday that I sang to you our love song
I sit at the end of my bed thinking about how you made me feel when you held me in your arms
Every morning and night I look over my shoulder to only catch a glimpse of your shadow
The work day takes up most of my time and energy, but when the moon is high
not even the temperature in the room can warm my aching heart
I try my best to imagine your gracious form sitting across the dining room
but I always waste God's glorious food with the second serving
Oh those wonderful memories I share with my mirror while curving my eyelashes
When I caress you silken pillow I dream of how beautiful you are now
But I wish I could have said goodbye or see you later
You were the other half of my heart
How can I ever fulfill it again?
The Lord made us one
I pray I can join you soon
Oh my love, where have you gone?

The authorities said that you vanished into thin air
Not a trace was left on the plane
just the roars and debris
They said they saw the brightest star that night
Gleaming with a smile
"My love, our dream has come true…
You will be joining me *soon*."

Singing

The perseverance of a child
The rhythm of the rope going round and round
Their hearts racing towards the mark
The constant beat of every step towards victory
Their smiles bloom up the towers
Children we hear your voice
The ball forms the perfect rainbow of life
But the shot is their success
Their joy calms even the heaviest of burdens
The laughter flows from soul to soul
Children we feel your love
The musical art form of dance
Swinging arms of praise shadows the rainy blessings
Swing higher, swing higher
The sky's their glory
Watch my instructors
Listen to the story
Learn the roots
Master destiny
Children we hear your song

Love

Chapter 6

God's Love

Spreads from universe to universe,
Planet to planet, hemisphere to hemisphere
Ocean-to-ocean, country-to-country, state to state,
City to city, street to street and…
He also knocks at your door, will you let Him in?

Changed

I remember doing all of those wonderful things to make the time pass by
I remember losing my soul in the crowd of temptation
The college life was oh so great
But I learned more than just earning a degree
I was blind, but now I see
This innocent girl raised in a Christian home
It was time for her to push through the sheltered walls of stability
No one, not even she knew the evil one slept close to where she rested
She was able to put up a front that she was a Christian during the day
But the promiscuous one came out at night
What was her problem you ask?
The man she once loved did not claim her

The love of the other fulfilled her aching heart
But just for a little while
The beginning ended and the "wonderful was gone"
The certificate in her hand but her heart never found
Many priests would listen and they told her where to find the answer
Shameful and depressed, but she finally kneeled down:
Repented
Jesus now sleeps close to where I rest
He continues to heal and reveal me to myself
I share this one testimony with you
Many more exist, but in due time…
I know His love for me…
He knocked ever so patiently at my door and I finally let him in.

Future Husband

Praying endless prayers night after night for you to come
waiting for our spirits to become one and to unite in perfect love
The one darling wandering out in this crazy world:
She desires for you to find your way into her heart
She has seen the wanna-be's and the shoulda-coulda-woudas
But the faith that she has in you outweighs them all
She daydreams of how wonderful you will be when you express your tears of joy
How you will tickle her soul when you try to justify your actions
How even the simplest things such as the smoothness in your stride
The way you will impress her with the never-have-done-before chores
Grooming in the mirror before her return
Sprinkling just a few drops of that cologne to make her senses go wild
How you say the right pet name to set the moment of flame
How spectacular you look in your favorite sweat suit
Gazing into your eyes, she sees the vision of your hopes and dreams of a better place
Only for her to stand by you proudly and gracefully hand in hand
Only *your* warm embrace could make her feel safe and comforted
Only your sweet kiss can set her mind at ease from trouble

When she does for a walk, sometimes she catches a glimpse of you.
Or even looking out of her window at night…
No one else can see you but her because you and her were meant to be
Her endless prayers are for you to be happy and when the time is right…
For her to be the best half of you than she could ever be

Future Wife

Praying endless prayers night after night for you to come
Awaiting for our spirits to become one and to unite in perfect love
The one true innocent sweetheart gliding through this dangerous world
He needs you to put together the puzzle pieces to his heart
He has glanced at the forgive-you-nots
He may have even past the once in a lifetime rejoices
But his yearning love for you has never phased
He fantasises about manifesting yours and his creations of joy
How you will tickle his soul when you try to be the head and him be the neck
How even the simplest things such as kissing the napkin after your favorite meal
The way you will amaze him with your confidence and strength as his lady
Beautifying yourself in the vanity before his return
Dashing a few drops of that special scent that would lead him across the hall
How your silence captures his mind of captivity
How glamorous you look in that simple, contouring black dress
Gazing into your eyes, he sees the vision of your love and compassion to those in need
Only for him to stand by you faithfully and boldly as every man for his own should
Only *your* comfort could ever make him feel secure

Only your sweet caress can set his mind at ease from pain and distress
When he goes for a walk, sometimes he thinks that he just passed you
Or even looking out of his rearview mirror at night…
No one else can see you but him because you and him were meant to be
His precious prayers are for you to be joyous and when the time is right…
For him to be the best half of you because you have completed him

The Wedding Band

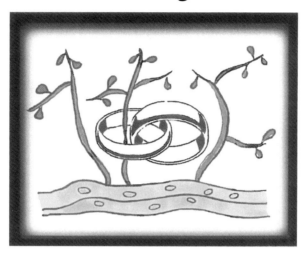

The grains of the seed are priceless jewels of hope,
waiting for the right harvest to emerge
The richest soils of the depth raptures its nature
The baby leaf comes up for a glimpse of the peaceful wind
Then another, sighing for the chance to be known
Thousands wishing to give life to the miracles
They all pray for the sun and holy waters to spring forth
For the Caretaker to spray away the pests with His nourishment
The tree of life thrives forward…
More divine and powerful than ever
But the season changes…
They scramble like animals to be untangled
by the deadly forces of the jungle
The struggle of hardships, the agony to be released
The boldness of the deep has begun to shed its pureness
The growth bows down its head in the name of shame
The beautiful heart-shape surrenders to darkness
Oh Lord, our Savior: when will freedom ring?

41

The briskness marks our smoothing texture
The constant smothering of these contaminated flakes
halts our dreams and our ambitions
But the faith of a grain of mustard seed conquers all
They touch their love with their spirits
They remember holding each other's hand on that special day
The circle of life was planted then and it will never end
The pain in our tips may have turned and withered away
But the calm of our storm always leaps new beginnings
The wrinkles of the past strengthens our core branches
Look at us now…
His spiritual guidance comforts us
His knowledge quenches our joy
Freedom you ask
Me, you and I are everlasting in mind, body and soul
Your rebirth has released your destination:
Yours is forevermore

The Little Boy

The Little Boy

The streets of rage tumbling down on my precious child
The inner city lights seem to be brighter from the madness of murder: It cries out to me
Their spirit becomes rigid with every abused substance
The souls are running ramped in the air tripping each other to get a lead on the road map
But there is one whom I truly adore: His markings bring forth the pain but yet salvation
Standing still, waiting for the light to turn red so he could finally walk.
The warlord grins at little Timothy when he sees the substance in his hand
Hand it over my son, he said.
My grammy, Timothy said, she's all I have
"I know that's why I will give you the money after your accomplishment"
The man I watch you kill did he have a grammy too? Timothy asked
"Don't worry about that know, they were our enemy anyway"
I still don't remember how I got here Master Joe
"You've been my son ever since your mother died from your birth…"
"I'm your father and mother now"
"Next time I will give you the honor to decease them"
This was the daily routine of the gang world
This was the only family Timothy knew but his future proved different
Even his caretaker could not understand the tattoos of a crown around his head
The sphere on his left torso and the cross in his right hand
Grammy would always say that the meaning would be revealed to Timothy at His time
Every Friday was the exchange of blood for money
Every Sunday evening was the preparation to conquer power
"My son it is time, are you ready for your first victory?"
The newborn, the newlyweds, new life perished
Slain in the darkness alley from the only conscience he knew
Pain in the midnight hour where I heard and answered last confessions
Frame was the word used to describe the corruption of innocence
Timothy was ten with the sword in his left hand
"Well done son," said Master Joe. Here is your money take care of grammy

Laying before him sick and deprived, but yet pain of wisdom
Grammy I have your medicine: he showed from his right with the cross
Endless tears flowing down her face from the bloody stain on his left hand
Grammy I have done a good deed: killing the tainted grants overwhelming wishes!
Said so my warlord, Master Joe who has shown me everything about this cruel world
And how we must fight to survive!
Oh Lord please forgive me for not teaching him thy ways correctly please give me strength!
Oh little rabbi (his nickname) I'm so sorry for the pain I have caused
I must tell you the truth about your markings before it's too late!
Your mother, Mary was born and raised in this same house, the city of Zion
Zion means holy land son and she was the caretaker of the children of this town
The children loved her for she feed and raised most of them, while their folks worked
She was a righteous woman my son, so much so that she willingly handed her life over
To the ones who your warlord proclaims to be outsiders trespassing on his land
He came into town manipulating the little ones with treasures and unclean substances
They would tend to their homes with their folks and sneak out late at night to meet the man who
claimed to be the answer to all their problems of poverty, money and success
Many if not all were lured in which is exactly what happened to you
Timothy, you were among those children some ten years ago
He made you believe that your people were evildoers and were making
you pay the price for their ignorance: when in fact he was the evildoer
Your mother was the most beautiful, faithful, honest hardworking woman in this town
She did the Lord's will each and everyday and prayed that the little sore in your head would heal
and you be made whole forever
That's why you can't quite remember son, but she loved you so much that she gave up her life!
My sweet Timmy (she clutched both of his hands)
Although my sight is gone I can still see all things, much better than ever
He tells all the children that their mothers died at birth but that's not true
She fought till the end: she was given a choice, to either have you or her killed for the believe of Jesus
Christ
She was slain for her believe to save you my son
The cross on your right hand helps you weigh the balance of good versus evil: good and bad (right or
left)
It signifies that for every right thing you do you shall carry your cross for his name's sake
The world hated him and they shall hate you as well
The crown circling your head reminds you of your salvation of everlasting life

46

The spear on your left side symbolizes his truth coming to light with the purging of his sanctified blood
The cause of our Lord's death was oh so devastating and brutal
But the effective beauty of the aftermath was overwhelmingly joyful
He saved us my son! He died on the cross for our sins so we may have everlasting life
Man tried to prevail against him but they always failed
You are the chosen one little Rabbi
But Grammy who is my father?
Your mother tried desperately to tell me that your warlord was a part of you
But I knew from the look in her eyes when you were born that he had been here before
The warlord is your father little Rabbi but by force
Oh no grammy!! Grammy!! He cried. He made me believe that the people here
Were our enemy and that him and I needed to slay them!
Oh grammy I have slain innocent blood! What am I to do?
There is such a thing as monsters that abide in human beings
The Lord does have his opposite, the devil but remember
He's just an influence and when you call on the name of Jesus, the enemy has no choice but to flee
Just ask the Lord for forgiveness and he shall set you free…
Oh my dear boy heaven has rejoiced over your confession and
the salvation of your soul…
It is time my boy, for me to abide in that sweet bosom that has given me peace
Don't worry my little Rabbi, I go to aid your mother with wonderful,
Priceless jewels of our God's love for you
But… Grammy! What about the medicine?
No need for it now my boy, the Lord has touched me and made me whole! I know see all things
The act was performed out of sin, but the beauty of you has set me free oh I love you so!
My spirit will be with you always
Oh Lord avenge thy little Rabbi and be his shield
Let him know that it was only you that brought him from a mighty long way!
Thy will be done
Standing there, complete silence: bittersweet tears flow down Timothy's face
He trembled ever so softly while putting his hands over his face
Falling down to his knees he cried… AAAAHHHHH!!! MOM-MM-Y!!
I heard a voice that could only come from the one I had my eye on when he first came from me
I held him tightly and promised him that I would never let go
The battle was about to begin: looking up at me with his disfigured, puffy eyes
I made his markings known… I washed, bathed, clothed and conformed his hair and feet

47

No weapon form shall prosper against you my son
(Knock, Knock, Knock)
He walked into the room where his mother-in-law lay
Timothy followed behind him
"I heard you scream my son and now I understand, I'm so sorry
But it was the name you screamed…that caught me off guard"
Father… she told me everything about my mother Mary and what you did to her
"Your grammy was very sick many people tell many fairy tales when their time is up"
NOOOOO!!! You killed my mother!! I know what these markings mean now
You didn't tell me because you knew it would destroy you and your so-called family!
I wish you were never my father… my real Lord will avenge me of you
"Oh, I see she laid that Christian crap on you… so you're all big and bad now huh, huh well are ya!
She turned you into the bastard son that I never wanted to have in the first place
You are no longer mine…."
I don't care I have always had a father who loved me no matter how I was made
"You better stop talking that mess boy; you know what happened to your mother!"
He drew his sword and began to strike him but little Timothy held up his right hand
Which revealed the cross and the shield reflected the sword away from him
He tried to strike again on his abdomen and the sword reflected again and again on his head
"What have you become! Who do you think you are!"
You will no longer control the future or me with my savior
Get behind me Satan… you are not welcome here ever again
Several weeks passed by and no one in the village had seen or heard
Of the warlord ever again, he left not a trace…
Some say he vanished because of the prince of Zion, Timothy
Some say he was standing still waiting for the light to turn red to cross the street
But he decided to run and a fatal accident struck him to his death
I know it was strange to parade about someone's passing
But everyone in the village knew the evil spirit that dwelt there
And that I would deliver them with my courageous knight…

Printed in the United States
126401LV00001B